JOHN FIELDER
CALIFORNIA
IMAGES OF THE LANDSCAPE

PHOTOGRAPHY BY JOHN FIELDER

WESTCLIFFE PUBLISHERS, INC. ENGLEWOOD, COLORADO

CONTENTS

International Standard Book Number:
ISBN 0-942394-13-5
Library of Congress Catalogue Card Number:
85-050035
Copyright: John Fielder, 1985
Designer: Gerald Miller Simpson • Denver
Typographer: Edward A. Nies
Printer: Dai Nippon Printing Company, Ltd.,
Tokyo, Japan
Publisher: Westcliffe Publishers, Inc.
P.O. Box 1261
Englewood, Colorado 80150-1261

First frontispiece: Morning clouds and salt water foam retreat the coast, Mendocino County

Second frontispiece: Morning light, Mono Lake, Mono County

Third frontispiece: Sword ferns drink from the wet forest floor, Klamath National Forest

Title page: Evening light, Big Sur, Monterey County

Right: Jeffrey pine cones, Mono County

PREFACE

There are some of us who are born curious. We delight in going just a few miles further on the mountain trail to get yet another perspective on a distant vista. We explore coastal forests that others are content to drive by, absorbing their smells and studying their patterns. We scramble to the top of desert sand dunes, wondering how the shadows will play upon the stark landscape from yet another vantage point.

We must see the unreachable ridge of peaks that lies, perhaps, around the next turn. We won't stop walking the beach until we've come to the last hidden cove, inaccessible below precipitous cliffs. We hope for bigger, more vivid patches of desert wild flowers.

For those with a passion for experiencing, California both frustrates and fulfills: lifetimes are needed to scratch its surface; yet what can be seen is so visually diverse that it is constantly stimulating.

I have spent two incredible years photographing the California wilderness for this book. Exploring boundary to boundary, I was witness to its amazing geologic, meteorologic, and biologic diversity.

The combination of crustal tectonics, vulcanism, and weathering has produced breathtaking scenes throughout the earth, but nowhere are the results more spectacular than in California. Every day of my two-year odyssey brought new satisfactions and new mysteries as I marvelled at the varied topography. I often moved from low desert through subalpine zones to coastal mountains within a few hours.

My photographic work began in early spring with a drive from Colorado across Arizona and over the Colorado River to the hot, relatively unexciting southeastern deserts of California. The previous winter had been one of the wettest in 100 years, transforming this usually parched, bleak landscape into a palette speckled with the fresh hues of countless wild flowers.

The Mohave and Anza-Borrego Deserts were a spectacular initiation for me. I was ecstatic to be photographing colors of the complete chromatic spectrum: reds of paintbrush, mauves of verbena, yellow of daisies. Often I was at my camera by 5:30 a.m., alone in the desert with the flowers and sun. I remember the incongruity I felt when the roar of a B-1 bomber prototype would fill the stillness.

I returned many times to the Mohave, but without its flowers it was unproductive for me as a photographer. The Anza-Borrego Desert between the Salton Sea and San Diego, however, with its canyons, arroyos, cacti, and magnificently colored rocks was always very productive.

Nearby Joshua Tree National Monument is home to thick forests of cholla cactus; I spent hours pulling the spines of their prickly fruit off my boots.

The Anza-Borrego desert is less than an hour from the town of Julian with its 5,000 foot altitude. This enormous difference is but one example of the marvelous instant transitions one makes all across the state from high to low, low to high, dry to wet, green to brown, warm to cold. Travelling towards Julian, I left behind arid lands for picturesque apple orchards and groves of gentle green eucalyptus.

To the north of the Mohave Desert lie the great basins and ranges that extend into Nevada. Arid mountains of reds, oranges, and browns are cut by canyons colored by the rich hues of the electromagnetic spectrum. Interspersed are dried lake beds of white saline materials, often with sand dunes. The most famous of these basins is Death Valley National Monument. Mesquite Flat Dunes is one of its most photographed areas; I took my share as well, but never achieved an individual interpretation.

The road between Death Valley and the Sierras is a roller coaster: From 300 feet below sea level, up over the 5,000 foot Panamint Range, down again to sea level for the Panamint Valley, up to 6,000 feet to cross the White Mountains, then down to Owens Valley at 4,000 feet.

From there a new visual feast began, as I was beneath the gaze of our country's second highest peak, Mt. Whitney, and its tall sisters of the Sierra Nevada Mountains.

The Owens Valley is dominated by what remains of Owens Lake. Since the early '30s, Los Angeles has used its cool mountain water to sustain a growing population. All that remains is a small saline lake surrounded by alkaline material still mined for its minerals.

My second trip to the valley was in October. I wanted to photograph the lake with the Sierra Nevada Mountains in the background. I could reach the water by following a five-mile gravel road built up above the soft lake bed.

I was four miles out when I glimpsed the water, with sunlight glittering on its surface: the conditions were particularly nice for a good image.

I continued ahead on this sandy, elevated road bed around to the side of the water. All of a sudden the Bronco stopped moving and began to quickly sink. Within 30 seconds gray mud was up to and over the bottom of the doors. The road bed was underlain with wet mud from the lake.

Not able to open the doors, I climbed out the back of the truck and assessed my predicament. There was no hope to winch out, so I grabbed a jacket and headed toward the old town of Keeler which I could see about six miles ahead.

What should have been a 90-minute walk took three hours: with each step I sank six inches into the loamy, dusty, lake bottom.

By nightfall my truck was out of the muck. It had been a long day, and I had no pictures to show for it — only a towing bill and blisters.

Two summers of excursions into a dozen different drainages from Whitney north to Mammoth Lakes and the Minarets Wilderness Area revealed alpine country that awed even a Coloradoan. These relatively young,

Shooting-star decorates the alpine landscape, North Fork Big Pine Creek, Sierra Nevada Mountains

9

uplifted, and sometimes volcanic Sierras are an endless panorama of palisades, glaciers, and massive granite displays. Yet, magnificent though their topography is, their beauty also comes from the delicate shapes and colors of paintbrush, shooting-star and cinquefoil wild flowers such as those I photographed by the North Fork of Big Pine Creek.

Working in alpine terrain is always sensually stimulating and physically challenging. At 12,000 feet, the temperature at sunrise, even in mid summer, is usually below freezing. My numb fingers could barely manipulate the view camera to capture the alpenglo on Mt. Ritter and the calm reflections on Cecile Lake in the Minarets Range. To see the Sierra's western slope meant lugging 95 pounds of gear and provisions over Mono and Paiute passes. Even with the loyal help of my friend Bob Newman and my brother Bill, a llama would be in order. Nor will I forget the Saturday morning I spent in line to buy a wilderness permit to hike one trail to gain access to one drainage, with no freedom to roam the mountains.

The images I recorded around Mt. Lassen and throughout the northern Sierras pleased me. More subdued than its southern counterpart, this domain boasts broad-forested slopes and spectacular evidence of vulcanism.

Fog moves in and out of the great National Forests of Six Rivers and Klamath, creating silhouettes of the denizens of the forests. The pines and firs could stand no taller anywhere on earth. Countless waterfalls cascade magnificently into the green rivers of the Eel, Van Duzen, and Klamath with their spawning salmon. Red-buds in spring paint pink along gray limestone shores. This was a difficult place to photograph in winter, with the cold and rain numbing my fingers; fortunately the same cold wet air would rejuvenate me by 6:00 a.m. for the next day's work.

My journey west to the ocean followed the rivers to their end where the rugged northern coast of California is revealed. My first view of the sea-swamped shores and the ruptured earth beaten by the unyielding force of the Pacific staggered me. I knew at once why so many great photographers have chosen to spend a lifetime along the California coast. The crags, sea stacks, and gray pebble beaches make this domain unique to any in the world.

Where forests of conifers don't come to the edge of the sea, great grassy fields color the coastal landscape. Driftwood from countless logging camps covers the beaches, just as purple lupine overwhelms eroded cliffs as summer arrives and the sea begins to calm.

And the redwoods! Their great forests were especially abundant from Philipsville to the Oregon border, although they stretched as far south as Santa Cruz. A light mist usually filled the chill January air. With dripping ferns at my feet, I often experienced a transcendent feeling as I walked through this silent sea of green, with its hints of red from the thick, dark bark. As the fog would lift and the sun backlit the forest, it made big black silhouettes of gigantic trees — great meat for the landscape photographer.

My migrations took me up and down the coast in summer, in winter, in spring, and in fall. Like a child, I basked in the wonder of it all: the mustard, yellow lupine and ice plants on shore; the waving seaweed and algae clinging to rocks offshore; and all along the grasses and marshes clustering beneath sand dunes.

The colors were exquisite. I marvelled at the sea stacks and tidal pools in morning light, and in the red sandstone cliffs set on fire by the evening light. The foaming surf left endless glittering patterns as it receded from taupe beaches.

I remember Pt. Reyes for its 100 m.p.h. winds, and Ana Nuevo State Reserve for its barking sea lions. Monterey County's Pt. Lobos is a bit overrated, but the drama of Big Sur can never be. Oftentimes my mind returns to the cerulean blues of coastal water, and great, nameless cliffs looming high above rocky shores. Many times I'd take five mile hikes along deserted sea sides, climb over promontories separating beaches, and then fear that high tides would leave me stranded, defenseless against the beach's fierce winds.

There is so much more that two years of experiencing California revealed: the golden hills, their greens of winter, Diablo Mountains, great madrone, eucalyptus, and cypress trees; sheep scattered across coastal bluffs; cowboys and cows up and down the hills east of the San Joaquin Valley, and infinite other sights.

The last day of my two year odyssey was spent at Mono Lake. I fitfully passed a frigid November night in the back of my truck, hoping for a morning with which to fruitfully end my great California adventure.

I awoke at 5:00 a.m., thoroughly chilled. I put on the camera pack, slipped on fingertipless gloves, a hat, and down jacket, turned on the flashlight, and slogged my way through the mud and brinish water at lake's edge. I was thankful that I'd loaded my film holders the night before.

By 5:40 a.m. I was surrounded by water and muck, fumbling in the dark of morning to open my pockets, and trying in vain to get the big camera set up on the tripod with the appropriate lens mounted. My fingers were numb and had to be warmed by my breath every 5 minutes, but within 15 minutes I was as ready as I ever would be.

With faint morning light I jumped from rock to rock, sometimes missing and landing in 2 feet of freezing water until I finally found the proper vantage. I pointed the camera, held my breath for the exposure, gripped the cable release with my numb fingers, and opened the shutter. Just at that moment, the California sky caught fire with the most dramatic sunrise I had ever seen.

At 7:30 a.m. I got into the truck and headed home to Denver. I knew that my first California portfolio was complete.

JOHN FIELDER

Klamath National Forest, Siskiyou County

COLOR

"I am stimulated by great chromatic diversity. California possesses this quality. Here, the camera becomes my paintbrush, the film dyes my oils, and the photographic paper my canvas. Color is an important reason why creating art with a lens is so rewarding to me."

Chromatic joy of lupine and the morning sky, San Mateo County

Greens of the California winter, Colusa County

Paintbrush proliferate in coastal fog, Big Sur,
Monterey County

Overleaf: Lupine drink from the morning mist,
Shell Beach, Sonoma County

Greens of winter along the Eel River,
Mendocino County

Cliffs of Big Sur, Monterey County

Sand-verbena in spring along the Salton Sea,
Imperial County

Leafing alder, Klamath National Forest,
Siskiyou County

The Alabama Hills and Mt. Whitney, Inyo County
Pond, Yosemite National Park
Overleaf: Autumn's Mountain Maple, Siskiyou County

Big Sur, Monterey County
Tidy-tips in the Trinity National Forest, Trinity County

Beach and cliffs, San Mateo County
Rainbow Ridge, Humboldt County

Shell Beach, Sonoma County
Ansel Adams Wilderness Area, Sierra Nevada Mountains

Redbud blooms along the Van Duzen River,
Humboldt County

Penstemon colors the alpine landscape,
Inyo National Forest

*Mt. Ritter reflects in a tundra pool, Ansel Adams
Wilderness Area, Sierra Nevada Mountains*

Oak above the San Luis Reservoir, Merced County

Ground water rich in sulfur sustains fecund grass,
Lassen Volcanic National Park

Low tide, Mendocino County coast

Layia in bloom, Mohave Desert

Winter rains drench the barkless madrone,
Humboldt County

Overleaf: Lupine fields, Pt. Reyes

Bluebonnet, northern Coast Range

*Alpine tarns reflect the unfiltered blue of high altitude
sky, from Piute Pass, Sierra Nevada Mountains*

Eel-grass colors the coastal landscape, Sonoma County

Autumn, Yosemite National Park,
Sierra Nevada Mountains

Vine maple, Autumn in the Salmon Mountains,
Siskiyou County

Vine maple, Spring, Tehama County

FORM

"Form is not just important to black and white compositions. It is one of the essential ingredients for creating an intense visual experience in color as well. I am particularly excited by the repetition of shape in nature such as the linear property of a grove of tall redwoods. Patterns in the landscape that appear too perfect to result from natural creation appear constantly to the vigilant eye."

Sequoia, Sequoia National Forest

Creek water, Yosemite National Park

In the Redwoods, Winter, Myers Flat,
Humboldt County

After the morning fog, Sonoma County coast
Low tide, Mendocino County

Shapes of Big Sur, Monterey County
Remains of forests scatter the beach, Humboldt County
Overleaf: Oak silhouettes against the cool morning sky,
Mendocino National Forest

In wet years, the desert floor accommodates great fields of Coreopsis, Mohave desert

The northern coast accommodates vast strands of weathered stones, Sonoma County

Early leaves on the Big-leaf maple, Humboldt County
Shapes of the coastal domain, Sonoma County

Evening-primrose, Ana Nuevo Reserve,
San Mateo County

Along Big Sur, Monterey County

Overleaf: Hills of Winter, Contra Costa County

Weathering into harmony with the natural landscape,
Salmon Mountains, Siskiyou County

Pines, Sonora Pass, Sierra Nevada Mountains

Sun Cups, Mono Pass, Sierra Nevada Mountains
Mud cracks, Death Valley National Monument

Mosses consume denizens of the forest,
Trinity National Forest

Oak and faint evening light, San Luis Obispo County

Overleaf: Alpine tarn, below Piute Pass,
Sierra Nevada Mountains

Quaking aspen trees, Toiyabe National Forest,
Sierra Nevada Mountains

Joshua tree, Joshua Tree National Monument

Sedge in pond, Ansel Adams Wilderness Area,
Sierra Nevada Mountains

Mesquite Flat Sand Dunes, Death Valley
National Monument

October ice, Yosemite National Park
Coastal erratics, Big Sur, Monterey County

Dendrites of the receding surf, Big Sur,
Monterey County

Above the San Joaquin Valley, Tuolumne County

In the Gabilan Range, Winter, San Benito County
Alder, Salmon Mountains, Klamath National Forest

MOMENT

"Some moments in nature have a special quality that makes them stand out. A diffused ray from the setting sun, the ominous dark of a threatening storm, or an early snowfall: Frequently light or weather changes the visual character of a landscape. These transitory moments demand my quick reaction. Perspicacity and luck contribute to the effectiveness of these images."

A solitary Bristlecone pine endures a frigid October snow, White Mountains

Winter rains entrap a fertile domain, Coast range
Clearing fog, Sonoma County coast
Overleaf: The rural landscape, Mono County

Motion at dusk, Sonoma County coast

*Pine and Douglas fir penetrate a lifting storm,
Trinity National Forest*

Green hills of Winter, Glenn County

High tide leaves proof of its surge, Big Sur, Monterey County

Oaks and a lifting fog, Rainbow Ridge,
Humboldt County

Sea foam, Trinidad Beach, Humboldt County

Overleaf: Mountain storm, Toiyabe National Forest

Turbulent winter surf erodes the northern coast,
Shell Beach, Sonoma County

The turbulence of a summer storm theatens
Mono Lake, Mono County

Oak in snow-laden fog, Six Rivers National Forest

First snow of Winter, Six Rivers National Forest,
Humboldt County

Morning silhouettes, Big Sur, Monterey County
Evening silhouettes, Trinity National Forest
Overleaf: Evening light, San Mateo County

Greasewood below afternoon storm clouds,
Owens Valley, Inyo County

Forming cumulus clouds, Sierra County

Eucalyptus drinks from the wet of dense fog,
Marin County

Salt-cedar endures another dry summer,
Anza-Borrego Desert

Evening patterns, Humboldt County

*Filtered light highlights barren boughs,
Salmon Mountains*

*Overleaf: Rabbitbrush and sagebrush before
impending showers, Mono County*

Early snow befalls the White Mountains and ancient
Bristlecone pine, Inyo County

Cypress, Pt. Reyes, Marin County

PLACE

"Certain photographs convey such a strong feeling
of place they almost transport the viewer to the site
of the scene, and give a transcendent feeling of
being in harmony with nature. These views are of a
limited landscape, perhaps beginning two feet in
front of the lens and ending twenty feet beyond."

Shadow Creek, Ansel Adams Wilderness Area,
Sierra Nevada Mountains

Pond, Marin County

Juniper, Toiyabe National Forest,
Sierra Nevada Mountains

Overleaf: In the Redwoods, Wood sorrel,
Humboldt County

On the coast, San Mateo County
By the beach, Sonoma County

Consumed by fecund mosses, in the Redwoods,
Humboldt County

Early Winter, Eldorado National Forest,
Sierra Nevada Mountains

Mustards of Spring decorate the landscape, Pt. Reyes,
Marin County

Colors and shapes, along the beach, San Mateo County

Overleaf: Shooting-star, Indian paintbrush,
and Cinquefoil, North Fork Big Pine Creek,
Sierra Nevada Mountains

At beach edge, Big Sur, Monterey County
Winter, Klamath National Forest

Pond, Lassen Volcanic National Park
Pine needles on pond, Lassen Volcanic National Park

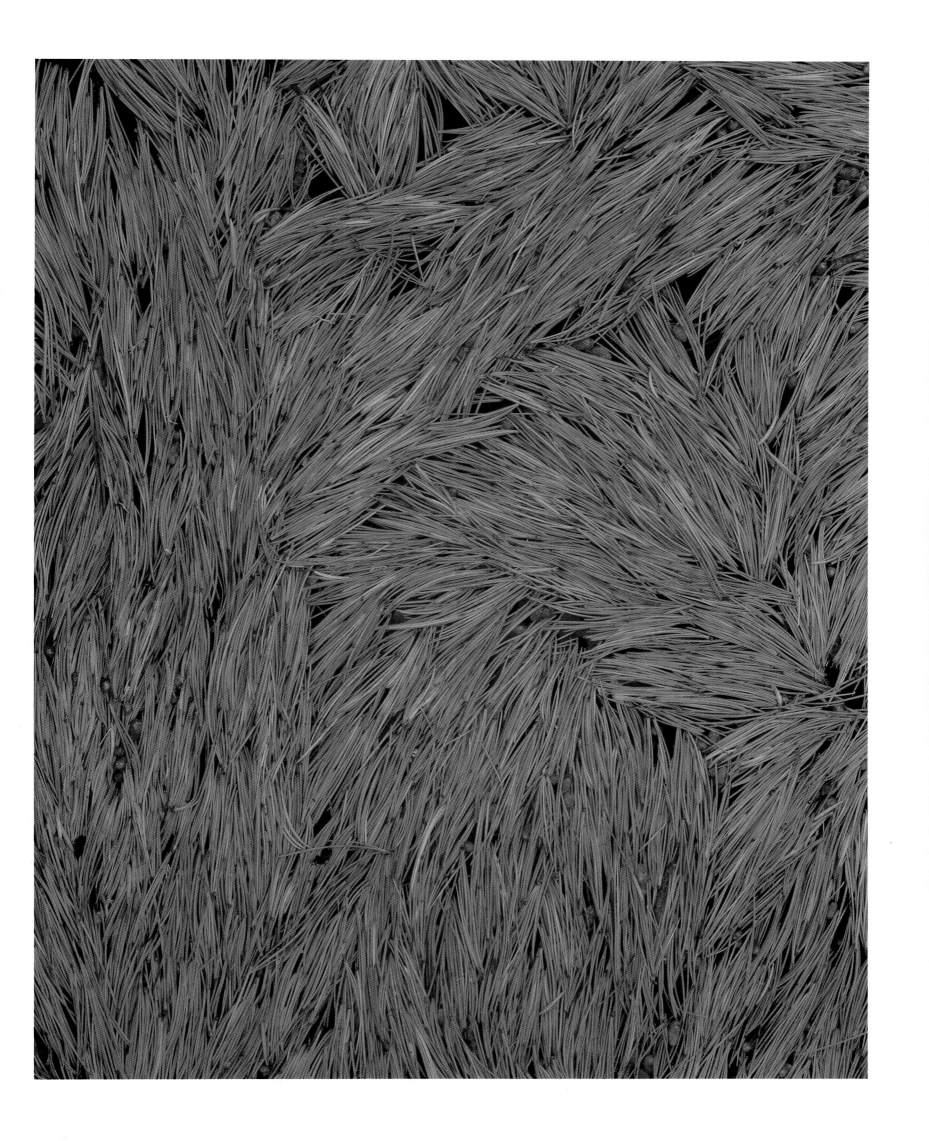

Alder exhibits its linear state, Pt. Reyes, Marin County

Rugged coast, Sonoma County

*Overleaf: Mid-Winter, northern
Sierra Nevada Mountains*

Sword fern and Lady fern in the wet,
Humboldt County

Sandstone carvings of the sea, San Mateo County

Oak, Klamath National Forest
Along the Eel River, Humboldt County

Beach-bur, Ana Nuevo State Reserve,
San Mateo County

Remains of summer, Tulare County

Abandoned domicile, Glenn County
Reflections, in the Redwoods, Humboldt County

Above the beach, Sonoma County
Lodgepole pine, Yosemite National Park

Leafing oak render the colors of Spring,
Mendocino National Forest, Colusa County

Clyde Minaret, Ansel Adams Wilderness Area,
Sierra Nevada Mountains

Snow-melt, below Piute Pass, Sierra Nevada Mountains

Owl-clover colors the alpine landscape,
Yosemite National Park

Overleaf: Infinite shapes, Sonoma County coast

MICROCOSM

"So much happens in the wilderness landscape beyond the reach of normal vision. Our inability to magnify what exists in nature's microcosms robs us of countless views of the natural world. The qualities of color and form take on new meaning in this world, so we must be perceptive if we are to understand and enjoy it."

Brown algae floats, along the beach, Sonoma County

Wood sorrel, Mendocino County

Broken shells, Ana Nuevo State Reserve,
San Mateo County

Ice plant, Pt. Reyes, Marin County

*Dead conifer, Toiyabe National Forest,
Sierra Nevada Mountains*

Overleaf: Pebbles, on the beach, Sonoma County

Creek-worn sticks, Alpine County,
Sierra Nevada Mountains

Brown algae, along Big Sur, Monterey County

Madrone tree trunk, Humboldt County
Forest floor, Toiyabe National Forest, Mono County

Frost on Big-leaf maple leaves, Salmon Mountains

Sycamore tree, Cleveland National Forest

Overleaf: Pine needles on hail stones,
Sierra Nevada Mountains

Sandstone, on the coast, Mendocino County
Brown algae, Monterey County

INFINITY

"Infinity is the last component that contributes to the intensity of an image. Images with a sense of infinity are often the ones that arrest attention, as they look far in the distance, straight ahead and from side to side. This characteristic is fairly simple: any majestic peak soaring into blue sky and reflected by a lake will do. Intensity, however, is only present when it comes from an emotion felt by the photographer."

Morning clouds on Mono Lake, Mono County

Overleaf: Clyde Minaret protects Cecile Lake, Ansel Adams Wilderness Area, Sierra Nevada Mountains

Oak and golden hills, San Luis Obispo County
Evening light isolates shapes of the rugged coast,
Sonoma County

South from Pt. Delgada, Humboldt County

Tarn, Ansel Adams Wilderness Area,
Sierra Nevada Mountains

Morning shadow, Mono County

*The remains of Bristlecone pine lay high in the
Ansel Adams Wilderness Area, Sierra Nevada Mountains*

Along Big Sur, Monterey County

*The low morning sun illuminates the landscape,
Mono Lake, Mono County*

Overleaf: Death Valley National Monument

Golden hills reflect colors of Summer, Merced County

*Green hills reflect colors of Winter,
San Luis Obispo County*

Rabbitbrush and Sagebrush endure the frigid
alpine Winter, Mono County

Similarities in shape, San Jacinto Mountains

Overleaf: Bulrushes penetrate cold water,
Owens Valley, Mono County

TECHNICAL
INFORMATION

The images within this book were made with a Wista 4″ × 5″ field view camera, using lenses of 75mm, 115mm, 150mm, 210mm, and 300mm focal lengths.

Ektachrome 64 transparency film was used exclusively. Yellow and red gelatin filters were used in cloudy and shaded conditions to correct for imbalances related to the blue dyes in the film. At times a polarizing filter was used to eliminate glare on water.

Exposures were calculated with a Pentax Digital 1° spot meter using both values in the landscape and a gray card. Apertures varied from f5.6 to f64. Exposures varied from 1/60 second to about 40 seconds. Gelatin filters were used to correct for reciprocity failure during long exposures.

The transparencies were separated on state-of-the-art laser scanning devices by the printer. Color reproduction was achieved with the goal of faithfully duplicating the image on film and accurately capturing the moment as it existed in time.